Teardrop

A poetry collection by Liv Adkins

FIRST EDITION

For my muses. You know who you are.

L.A.

<u>I Have Only Known One Rainbow.</u>

Good morning, children!

Today we will learn about

C O L O U R !
Some of us are PINK!
We are popular even if we don't know why. We sparkle and glimmer and sing. We catch our breath when the pretty boy onstage starts dancing. And if you wrong us, you will regret it.

Some of us are BLUE!
We smile at sunsets even though our pictures won't come out. We never wake before ten. We have feet licked by the ocean and hair blown by the wind. And if you make us cry, you will never be able to forget it.

Some of us are ORANGE!
We are rare and strange. We always know another orange when we see one, and we are the best friends an orange could have. We smile with all our teeth. And if you push us away, you will never get us back.

Some of us are GREEN!

We never stop wondering and we never stop loving. We are excited by the trees and the grass and the eyes of a girl we aren't quite brave enough to befriend. We laugh a little too loud and trust a little too much. And if you hurt our hearts, you may never be forgiven.

Some of us are VIOLET!
We love our own hands and faces and bodies. We understand things others don't and live in a world they may never see. We believe in magic and poetry and string instruments. And if you knock us down, we will stand up and push you back.

Some of us are YELLOW!
We know the moon like the backs of our hands and never avoided looking into the sun. We keep daisies in our bones and marigolds in our eyes. When we fall asleep, we dream of flight. And if you frighten us off, you will always wonder what could have been.

Some of us are RED!
We chase butterflies and count ants. We don't fear pain. We know how to forgive and how to earn forgiveness. And if you anger us, we will make sure you don't do so again.

About a Boy.

He will probably be alone in old age
because he is
unstable
so now, he reasons,
now is the time for fun.
Now is the time for laughter and
adrenalin and
far too much of the risk he enjoys so fully.
Now is the time to do what he loves
to study his passions and
forget the rest.
Now is the time to hurt others,
for later, when his youth fades,
there will be time enough
for apologies.

<u>Bright Little Sun.</u>

i. I adore her. It's in her aura- I have trusted her since the beginning and I will love her until the end. When she laughs your troubles disappear.

ii. There's a certain aesthetic to being her friend. It's pastels and walking confidently and slowly down the street and smiling even if you don't think your smile is becoming. I wish this aesthetic would follow me home. I wish she could come along with it.

iii. The four of us are too loud and too fun and not at all the cool kids, but I like us the way we are. I get the feeling everyone else does, too. We are the sun, the moon, the stars, and the sky. She is the sun.
The rest of us fall in nicely.

iv. Her heart is probably the size of Jupiter.

v. When you take the weight off her shoulders she looks as if she might float away. There's so much joy in her round, beautiful face that I nearly cry.

<u>Never Let A Boy Get You Back Into Radiohead.</u>

I've always loved brown eyes and
I couldn't be more relieved to know yours aren't
blue.
I told myself I wouldn't love you.
But really, after all the hailstorms,
Best Friends is as much an I love you as soul-
mates.
Best Friends is brighter than the rainbows of a
million sun showers.

It's so hard to write a love song when you're ter-
rified of love.
It's so hard to write a love song when the way I
love you isn't what love songs are for.
It's so hard to write a love song when I don't
know if you'd leave the radio on to hear it.

And I'm not the type- I better not be the type to
smile for a scrubby beard and pajama pants and
heavy brown eyes and I BETTER not be the type
to smile for Sir Galahad.

But hey, you make me laugh.

<u>Maybe Radiohead is Good, Actually.</u>

He gave me apples and cranberries.
Apples and cranberries, like an autumn harvest
in an old chapter book.
Apples and cranberries, like my favourite juice
when I was twelve.
Apples and cranberries, and it wasn't just my
low blood pressure that made me dizzy when he
said he was my boy.

I hate apples and cranberries.
Sometimes loving someone makes everything
seem beautiful.

I walked him to his room and I talked almost the
whole time but
It was okay because he seemed to care.

I said it would be his fault if I fainted and he
laughed.
He mouthed something to me as if he wished we
could keep talking and
I smiled and nodded as if I understood.

I didn't understand
Why my heart got so light at the little things,
At apples and cranberries, but
I stopped giggling four and a half years ago and
He's got me giggling again.

I guess there's nothing wrong with trusting and
loving a boy like that,

A boy with warm brown eyes and
An openness to friendship and
The best smile in the world, and
Like I said, he makes me laugh.

John Wodehouse Looks Out.
Portrait of John Wodehouse, 1764, by Pompeo Batoni

Wodehouse leans against stone grey and firm as
a new world,
A hero.
'Adzooks!' thinks he, 'behold that game pullet!'
She is tallow-breech'd and supple in the apple-
dumpling shop,
Ripe for picking.
Her face is christened by a baker, sweet and
wide-eyed.
Wodehouse smirks his satisfaction.

Twenties-young and fine is he,
Eyeing the pintle-merchants as they pass.
His eyes rest on a gentle maid, a boisterous sir,
many a fine youth,
Drinking up their auras.
Wodehouse may be half seas over, but he feels
Fresh and young,
And were he to open his mouth any wider, a
lustful cry would sure escape.

His gentleman's wear bluer than the grey sky
above, his lace and accents of gold
crying out his dignity, Wodehouse peers confi-
dently out.
The youth around him may be fair,
But Wodehouse knows he is the fairest.
He may have eyes for them, but there is no
doubt all eyes will one day be on him.

At eighty-three he will be no more than a body,
His immortalized youth six decades gone,
And he, returned to earth and forgotten.

Caterpillar Girl.

The little
girl
with the polka-dot bruises on
her arms
and knees and
everyplace asked me,

"Why don't they love me?"

(and I could
not answer but) I said
that they were
Blind
to her beauty because
she is a caterpillar now and
it takes someone special to see a butterfly
inside a
caterpillar's skin
and she said

"Maybe so but
nobody calls a caterpillar-"
and the next word
she whispered to
me because
she's too gentle to say
it out loud.

slug.

in the tumble-stream mountains
in the dewey, mist-eyed afternoon
the slugs
raise their heads to the sky/

in a chemistry classroom so humid-awful
her palms stain the table
the-girl-i-used-to-be thinks her mind must be a
slug:
slow   ugly   screaming silently   writhing to-
ward nowhere
she holds back tears
picks at a zit/

in the blue-soft air
the slugs are trembling
it is springtime now
the-girl-i-used-to-be notices them
thinks they are precious
yet as she kneels down to whisper
all-things-grow
she loses herself/

she loves the slugs
she wants to
she lifts a stick from the needle-soft ground
tenderly opens a slug with it
it was a wondrous slug
yellow as pus
slick as water-stone
a creature with a soul/

the-girl-i-used-to-be stifles a sob
she has betrayed her own kind
taken a life/

for once she thinks
there might be a god
for only something as terrible as a god
would craft a slug
to let it die/

the-girl-i-used-to-be buries the slug
her slug
prays for forgiveness
the greatest being she has ever known
a buried stain.

Sonata For Two Mediocre Cellists.

In December, I was not in love. There was someone I looked at and pictured under a willow tree, smiling at me and pushing the curls from their face, and there was someone I pictured sticking their tongue out at our wedding, and there was someone I gave all my affection, leaving none left over even for myself. But they sent me on a voyage through a convoluted sea of thoughts, and when I reached the end, I found it was the same as the beginning, and all I had was a lost year. In December, my heart was broken, but I was not in love.

In July, I was not in love. There was someone who made me smile and helped me laugh and taught me how to love myself again, and there was someone I trusted with all my secrets and all my pain and all my love, and there was someone I imagined sharing a flat with in New York City as we struggled to find a way onto Broadway, tired but happy. But he was only my friend when it was convenient, and he took all I gave and paid it back in such a way that I always had less but always felt indebted to him, and he decided that he simply didn't need me, simply didn't want me when the month ended. In July, my heart was broken, but I was not in love.

Now it is a new December, and I am not in love. I love you. But I am not trying to tell myself that I'm in love. I am not trying to chase you down and hold your hand. I am not afraid to mess up and lose your love, because I know you are my friend, and I know where I stand, and I know that you will love me even if I'm less than perfect.

I have made a myriad of mistakes and woken up from so many nightmares that some nights I am still afraid to sleep. But you were not a mistake. And you are not a nightmare. You are what I have woken up to.

Down bow on open C.
Silence.
Applause.

The View From Washington.

I want to take you in my arms and hold you so close I can feel your heart beating and I want to bury my face in your neck and know everything will be okay in the end.
I want to look into your eyes and see that same stars that are in mine.
I want your fingers intertwined in mine as we stand on a rooftop and look at the stars and I want to tell you,
Sure, the stars are beautiful, but it's people like you that make them worth watching.
I want to give you all the love that is in my heart and I want you to give me all the love that is in yours.
I want to know that I make you smile, and I want you to know that when I am tired and old, your name will still be all it takes to put the light back in my eyes.
I want to play with your hair and kiss the top of your head and smile softly and laugh fully and live completely, and I want to smile and laugh and live   with you.

<u>Mind-Map in B Major.</u>

i. Camisole camisado camouflage camel Camille
Camilla Camillo (armadillo) Cameron Camryn
(ah, that's it!) campground campaign camera
chimaera chim cheroo (not now) came come
command commando commander computer
compete complete (these words don't even start
with cam anymore)-
Anyway, we call (called?) her Cami.

ii. A rose is a rose is- Rosencrantz, my love, a
coin that lands heads, Rosencrantz and Guilden-
stern are dead, Rosencrantz and Guildenstern
are wed, Rosencrantz and Guildenstern- mis-
read, mislead, dark red, dark green, and scene!
...What, Rosencrantz dead, and I, Guildenstern,
gutted, gaunt, grievously alone, and what of it?
("I wanted to make you happy.") If one should
live it should never be Guildenstern, but Rosen-
crantz, rosy-cheeked, reliable, rhetorical, radiant
Rosencrantz, not I! Never Guildenstern! If both
should die- if both are dead- if Rosencrantz
should die as well- if Rosencrantz should die- if
Rosencrantz, oh Rosencrantz, wherefore art thou
Rosencrantz? Deny thy letter and refuse thy
name, or, if thou wilt not, be but sworn my love,
and I'll no longer be Guildenstern, still alive, but
Guildenstern who died of love by thy side.

iii. The far and so bright stars are so.

They are small, it seems, until you realise that you are small, but you are looking at it backward.
I, standing, am beneath them, crystalline!, and in gazing awe at glow (their).
They vanquish the night! Soft light that I see, I am in love!
My love Yet before quenched is - the sun - alas, come to blind me will.

iv. Call me Ishmael. Call me a friend of Cami. Call me Guildenstern. Call me a seeker of truth. Call me a seeker of love. Call me Arnold, call me Connor, call me Oliver, call me Jack, call me Emmie, call me Bert but never Herbert, call me what you will but know I am More than stardust, More than letters on a page, More than a squishy banana in summer, More than the peach-player who paid for your pastry, More than Enough. And call me back. (End on the I chord, let it resolve, but hold the pedal down so the sound never dies.)

My Brother's Tie.

You said I was
handsome
and I nearly cried and
for the rest of the night my head
was full of bees and my
heart
was full of that familiar ache
like fairy lights and love
but also like loneliness.
You said I was handsome and
I thanked God (or
whatever's up
there) that I wasn't
in love with
you
because if my best friend can
summon that many
bees
who knows what wasps love
could conjure?

Maybe the Void Will Listen.

i. !!!!!!

ii. I don't want to think about you anymore and I
don't want to feel this way like Christmas lights
like I'm glowing like somebody set me on fire
and I'm inside out and I love you I love you I
love you I love you and I don't want to love
anymore because everything I love is taken
away all the gold and the pink and the cool
lemonade won't exist anymore when the leaves
turn into the grass and I LOVE YOU

iii. I wish I had a way to say the words I feel in
my hands without scaring you away forever.

iv. My brain is so full of noise it's like a dream
but the dream is made of
bees of bees of bees of
bees!
and there's so much   s t a t i c
in my ears

v. We can do anything, or we could, maybe, if I
was less afraid and you were-
well-
I don't know, but SOMETHING
something concrete (something---not bees,)

vi. My mouth is open and my brain is screaming
but I am silent. That's my problem, isn't it? I'm
always

s i l e n t

vii. I refuse to stop loving you. I refuse to stop caring with all my energy.

viii. I will miss you if you disappear. Please stay with me, firefly. Please light up my midnights.

ix. Goodnight. I hope to see you there.

The Void Was Definitely Listening.

i. This time, I am the bird. I am the one whose song is light and happy and beautiful. I am the one who can fly.

ii. I love you and I'm not ashamed. I'm not afraid. And I don't feel like a fool. The bees and the static are gone, Starshine. Now there is only love. I love you. I love you, I love you, and I want to continue to love forever and I want to scream so loud the stars and the coral can hear, and when I scream I want to scream together.

iii. I am not silent anymore.

iv. Some things can stay. The pink and the lemonade can stay even if the gold does not.

v. Let me say it one more time- I love you. I love you with all my energy.

Just Another Stream-of-Consciousness Poem.

The music is playing and I wonder if the elephants can hear it. I wonder if you can hear it, Starshine.

I tell you I would take a bullet for you and you ask what you did to deserve that. I do not know. Maybe we thrum at the same wavelength. Maybe that's why I've loved you since I met you. Maybe that's why I used to get so afraid I would lose you- because people who thrum at your wavelength make you giddy, and they make you happy, and sometimes they make you cry until you can't breathe, even if they don't mean to. I believe you didn't mean to. I love you more every hour.

There's a girl I know and I wish things would go right for her and I wish I could get away from her because I don't think I can take care of her much longer and I don't think I can take care of myself very well when she's involved.

I worry sometimes, Starshine. You are going to find your greatness. I know you are. I hope you are. I worry you will outgrow my love. I worry everyone will. I worry I will be nothing but a girl who likes girls and a girl who looks at the moon and a girl who, despite all the love in her heart, is staggeringly alone.

It's then that I remember we are children. No. I am a child. You are barely bigger, but it's difference enough.

Buses may skid on black ice, and buses may not make the turn, and children may scream, but in the end it makes little difference. Each voice can change the world. The entire world cannot change the cosmos. The entire world cannot change a single man.

My problem is I don't have a dream. I have too many passions and too many fireflies to share them with. I have too much excitement and not enough direction, and I'm going to burn out like a candle on a soft white Christmas cake.

I want to love and be loved and trust and be trusted and never say goodbye. Good night, perhaps. But never goodbye.

For a year I considered you Gone. For a year I feared our next meeting. I never want to fear again. I never want to lose the friend I found in you.

Some of us are pink and some of us are green and that won't stop us from thrumming at the same wavelength. I know this. I hope this.

Some people hurt you and you remember them forever as the one who hurt you. Some people cannot be forgiven. Some people will smile every time they see you and only flip you off once they think you're not coming back. Don't let it stop you from coming back. Every year they will smile. Every year you will be stronger.

I love the violins. I love them almost as much as the cellos. I used to love the strings as a whole- I used to love the basses until the boy who swore and snarked and grabbed my little lion's heart right out of her chest ruined them. I used to love the violas before the first one sneered at us and made us feel inferior and in-dignant. I will never stop loving the cellos, and I will never stop loving the most beautiful girl in the world.

Oh, her voice is like clean linens and a comfortable couch in a tent on a beach. Which of us is not breakable? Which of us is not called by the chording player piano? Which of us is not ready to forget?

I am not ready to forget. I am breakable, and I am dancing as we speak, but I hope I never forget.

We will all die someday, firefly. There is no forever. You have taught me this. I do not be-lieve in forever. But if there must be an end, it behooves us to enjoy the days we have. Let us run, firefly! Let us dance!

The Void Is a Liar.

i. It's not static this time. It's not bees, either. This time it's a pain in my chest. I think it's my heart that hurts. I'm almost certain it's my heart that hurts.

ii. The pink and the lemonade are gone. They will be forever. I believe in forever again. I believe in myself, too. What I don't believe in is (you).

iii. I don't love (you). I never did. That was infatuation, (darling), and it's gone now. I would never take a bullet for (you), and I would never call you Starshine. Goodbye. Maybe someday (you) will realise what (you) lost.

iv. Real love lasts forever. I know this. I hope this. What (we) had was not real love. I know this. I don't have to hope.

v. Goodbye.

<u>shakespeare Knew what he was doing when he wrote r&j.</u>

god,
listen,
n i know that i say this 2 much,
bcuz by now u sometimes quote me,
sometimes u say it w me,
but can u BELIEVE,
n jus bear w me bcuz its so much 2 take in,
o my GOD can u believe it when i say-
Juliet was 13.

<u>A Short Story in Verse.</u>

They call her Magpie, though the reason has long been forgotten. She is very small in almost every way, and she is slave to none but the wind.

They call him Sammy, though the reason has yet to be discovered. He is tall and strong and never smiles because he has seen so many nightmares that he doubts if there is good left in the world.

She is twirling and leaping when he finds her. She sees his face and falls. The toadstools laugh. He does not catch her.

He is confused by her. He thinks she is beautiful, but he is not attracted to her. Something in the movement of her hair and the proportions of her limbs convinces him she is not human in the same way he is, or, perhaps, at all. He takes one step forward and reaches for her. Their hands touch and he gasps.

She does not know him, but she knows everything about him.
"Sammy," she whispers, her tree-bark hair quivering behind her in the breeze. She smiles and lets go of his hand and runs far away. The trees whisper rumours of her destination. All but one are wrong.

He falls to his knees as her hand leaves his. He is cold and tired and ready for anything but what has just happened. He follows her, the leaves crumbling beneath his feet and the wind blowing hard on the backs of his human legs.

She knows she is being followed, but she is not afraid.

"He has never hurt without reason," she says. The stones do not believe her. She slows, but the wind presses her forward.

He is almost out of breath, and the birds know this. He wonders if he should stop. The wind tickles his ears and whips his open shirt. He runs faster.

She wants to be found. She is a small, human bird, and she is curious. The curiosity splashes over her like a breath of fresh water, dripping from her chin and ears as she struggles against her invisible master. The sharp grasses are worried.

He has been running for too long, and he is burning and sore. His skin is cold and his muscles are melting. This skin cannot hold him much longer. Then, for precious seconds, he catches a glimpse of that same tree-bark hair, and he knows he will run as long as he must to find the dancing girl who knew his name.

The wind is cross. It hisses in her ear.

"A good bird does not fly into the wind."
She, too, is cross. She pushes her hair behind her
small head and puts her small hands on her
small waist.
"This one does."

He sees her slowly walking toward him.
He is confused by how slowly she moves, how
determined her gait is. Surely the wind cannot
hold her back. He is running as fast as he can
now. He tries to go faster and falls. The toad-
stools chuckle quietly. She does not catch him.

She narrows her dark eyes and moves
faster. She sees blood on the leaves below him,
blood on his broken lip.
"Sammy."
She reaches for him.
"Sammy!"
The wind blows her away and discards
her. He watches from the ground. He is fright-
ened and alone. The toadstools are not laughing
anymore.

She tumbles through the air and wildly
scrambles for control. The wind drops her and
she slides on the leaves. She is torn, soiled, and
silent. Tears cut tiny riverbeds in the dirt on her
wind-reddened cheeks. The sharp grasses whis-
per with sorrow that they were right.

He rises to his feet with great difficulty.
He can hear his brother calling him.

"Come on home, Sammy. I miss you."
But he knows it is the wind, the cruel, fickle
wind putting these lies in his ear. He loves his
brother so very much. But he is on a mission.

She is still crying, but now she cries tears
of anger and determination. Her sun-freckled
skin has been slashed and dirtied, but she does
not feel the pain. All she can feel is that odd sen-
sation as what used to be a curiosity becomes a
raw, hungry need. She cannot walk on one leg.
The trees reach out their branches, and she leans
on them.
She is not like other birds.

The sharp grasses point against the wind,
and he follows them. The toadstools watch,
amazed. He is growing very weak, and he is
growing very close. The wind blows harder
against his face. He curses it and pushes for-
ward.

The stones help pave the way for her sin-
gle hopping foot.
"She hops like a magpie," says one.
"She is a magpie," says another.
"No, she is more than just a magpie," says
a third. "She is special."
She reaches for a tree, but she misses. She falls
forward.

He sees her hopping toward him and runs to her. The trees, as all trees do, have roots. He trips and falls forward.

They catch each other.

She looks different up close. He looks at her eyes and they remind him of the moon. He looks at her face and she reminds him of no one but herself. She smiles, and he is happy.

He, too, looks different up close. He looks more like a boy and less like a man. She is unsure of why, but she thinks it is his eyes. He has puppy dog eyes when they are not narrowed in confusion or anger or determination or fear. She likes his eyes.

"They love each other," says one stone.
"Yes," says another, "but they are not in love."
They are both correct.

The hardened boy takes the precious broken bird on his back and carries her to safety. Her small fingers point the way. He stays with her through the peaceful, still night. She is not afraid.

When they wake, the sky is hundreds of shades of pink, a watercolour canvas behind the black trees. She tries to stand but cannot. She takes his hand and hops next to him. He trusts her. He knows she will not fall.

Together, their black silhouettes disappear into the forest. The wind is still. The sharp grasses are no longer worried.

Musings in the Small Patch of Trees the City Calls a Forest.

i. Alone.

ii. The stars look so small from here.

iii. I am insignificant, in the grand scheme of things. I am the small one.

iv. Sometimes I forget I exist. At these times, I am at peace.

v. Still.

vi. Waiting. Hoping. Mars is dim tonight, but Venus is brighter than a cat's eye.

vii. The city is loud and bright and busy and it makes my eyes ache. The trees are gentle and raw and pure and they make my heart ache when I am away from them.

viii. I have four limbs and no branches.

ix. Ursidae.

x. Look at the entire forest. No one can. Every-one must.

xi. As I grow older, I grow more foolish. I start to wish for a wife or a husband. I start to wish for children and a bed in a room in a home in the city.

xii. I am sitting on my bed in my room in my home in the city when I become wise once more and realise I am not, in fact, sitting in my home. I am just sitting, sitting on a bed in a room in someone else's home, in someone else's life, in the city.

xiii. The trees have not forgotten me.

iv. I have four limbs, no branches, and more hope than I've felt in many, many years. Mars is in the same sky as Venus, and they are both brighter than a cat's eye.

Third Grade.

My dad says every story I tell takes place during
the third grade.
He says every memory, every fairy tale, every
little bit of childhood that I choose to remember
has a 3 stamped on it in red ink, that I don't
speak of anything before or after.
He could be right.

Or it could be that it was in third grade that
the chipmunk-ugly boy told me I couldn't be his
friend and
 called the other third graders idiots and the
dark blank twins hung upside down
and spoke in jeering taunts and the tall,
slim, beautiful girl with curls like Jupiter
(because it's always curls isn't it)
just silently
nodded along. Her name was
Jennifer.
I wanted to like her so desperately,
back in third grade, and again in seventh grade
when she was even taller but
her makeup was smudged on purpose so it
looked like she'd been
crying even when she hadn't been and I realised,
hey, then nobody knows when you have,
but back to third grade, when I would sing to
myself
during recess because I had no friends but I
loved the thought of

composing an opera and starring in it, back in
third grade when
the boy with the parakeet eyes
looked at my neighbourhood-corner friend (her
curls were really something too) and told her
that he thought I had a crush on him- I did, but
that didn't matter, what mattered was that he
knew- and either way that might've been fourth
grade-
in third grade when I went into the hallway cry-
ing because I used the wrong form of "they're"
and I wasn't used to not being the best
except that might've been second grade? in third
grade when I scraped my knee
and started crying but
I wanted to be a boy so bad
that I tried to keep it quiet and I refused to tie
my shoes
in third grade when my teacher made us
 do that funky-monkey-gallon-of-sass dance and
my self esteem said no but
my need to please said yes
and all I'm trying to say is I may have no sense
of when but I'm almost sure
 that third grade was one hell of a year although
as a third grader id never say
 hell id say h-e-double-hockey-sticks because
thats what my best friend from first grade-ish
would say but i swear
at least some of this happened in third grade
  !!! ! !!!! !
… And besides, I have some wild stories from
sophomore year, too.

<u>The Forest.</u>

The forest, he reasons, is the purest place there is, and who would disagree? He leaves the path and walks in line with the gentle breeze, the trees whispering their magic under its tickling hand. Birds see him, hear fallen twigs snap beneath his heavy, human foot, and the birds are afraid.

They chatter warning
he comes

for who could trust
he comes!

a human?

The sun filters, warm, through the leafy rooftop, and the forest sighs. The ground is solid, cracked, and honest. He turns slowly, in love with the beauty his fathers destroyed.

He comes!
Beware!
He comes!

And suddenly he knows, he can sense that he is not welcome here. I am a good man, he wills the forest to believe. He puts his arms out to his sides and praises the trees.
I, he thinks, *can be trusted.*

He comes.
He lies.

But who

could trust

a human?

He lies.

He lies!

<u>The Forest, Part Two.</u>

His face is in his hands because he is crying. He
has been rejected before, by boys, by girls, by his
father's cold stare, but never did he think that
the wise, oaken coils which ensnared his heart in
childhood could grow thorns, never did he
doubt the forest's love.
The vines that once had been a playground now
wept and drooped at his touch. Mr. Robin in his
feathered suit had sung for him in childhood,
but now all birdsong was warning.

Look out!
Get away!
He comes!

The trees cannot trust him. They moan and sigh,
so powerful, so helpless against man's cruel
sword. The forest is afraid. He, too, is afraid, but
not of the forest. He is afraid of
himself
for if the forest cannot trust him, what monster
must he be? He is a murderer of beauty, just as
all men never should have become. And now the
birds are not alone in wondering
who

Look out!

could trust

He comes!

a human.

Rules.

He has said all I need to hear, and so I stand and walk away. I do not need him, and now I no longer want him. He was good to me, in his way, but I could never be satisfied by his side.

If you give a mouse a cookie, you will have one less cookie for yourself.
If you give a man a gun, you will have one less man.

I sigh, and my breath paints a picture in the cold. I see my mother's face. Now I see nothing. My fingers are numb, useless sticks on my hands. I bend my thumb, but I do not know how.

If a bird flies south, he will be warm. If a man flies south, he might see the bird, but he might not. There are rules. The rules are secret.

If a fish swims miles below the surface, in the darkest moaning crevices of the earth, for even under the ocean there is earth, then the fish will learn to live there. If a bird swims beside the fish - well, a bird will not. There are, as I have told you, rules.

If nature and man are one, then both can grow, both can be happy, but perhaps that is breaking the rules. If not, then man is a fool. But we know that. We have known that for a very long time.

He and I were friends. That is all. Being more would have broken the rules. It would, perhaps, have made me happy, but perhaps it would make the bird happy to swim so deep, and perhaps it would make the trees happy to pull up their tangling, knotted roots and walk, and perhaps none of us are powerful enough to break the rules without breaking ourselves.

If Ross and Frank are in love, they could be happy. But if Ross is in love and Frank is in love but Frank is in love with the girl who is missing, then no one is happy but James, and nobody likes James anyways because James is an airhead. James knows he is an airhead. James, for whatever reason, is proud.

If you give me a flower, I will become flustered and look at you with awe and perhaps pity, but if you give me your friendship I will grow to love you. Either way you have my attention.

There is paint on my hands. I adore it. Someday I will be married with paint on my hands and paint on my face and maybe even paint on my clothes, and they will think I am beautiful because they will love me, and I will love them, and when I kiss them I will get paint on their face, too, and we will laugh.

I paint my life, and I can fit all of it on one canvas. It is beautiful, so beautiful that one might not notice the sad parts and the fact that the corners have been lopped off. It is very beautiful, but it is not perfect. Nothing is, or was, or will be. I wonder if that is one of the rules. I hope it is. Once you see something perfect, you know you will never see anything better.

Somewhere, a rabbit is crying.
Sometimes, I cry too.
The rabbit is my friend. If you give a rabbit your friendship, it will become afraid. I do not blame it. A rabbit and a human are not the same. And there are rules.

<u>Eclipse.</u>

We could fit in the palms of giants as
we stretch like dancers and we
will not
give up.

All of us are reaching for the sun, aren't we?
We're all just reaching for the sun.

We're praying to a god we don't believe in be-
cause it's better than admitting there's nothing
left and we're gonna
die young
because we don't know how to
      STOP!!!!!
!

      ! ! !
     embrace the

           silence
it's like a waltz except we're drowning and the
water is sweet like the moans of a cellist (of the
cello as well) and maybe we can't breathe but we
can fly---!

We are all just
reaching
for the (r e a c h i n g   for the)
sun.

Precision.

We are working as one because it's what we know. We are on our hands with our feet in the air and maybe as one unit we can slow the growth of the roses in our bones. We all have our roses. Some of us have blackberries, too, and it's only the people without them who can taste their sweet juice.

It's only when we reach the sun that we realise the heat
is killing us.

Hold my hand and say good night.

Good morning, perhaps.

And reach.

<u>Broken Things.</u>

We could pretend there is nothing else. We could find a spot, alone, and sit and just talk, just me and you, our young, sweet souls and the gentle air around us.

In a perfect world, you'd be holding my hand and maybe even squeezing it. But this world is far from perfect, and we are broken.

Even broken things can heal.

Hope is so fresh and new and kind, and she takes my hand and she takes yours and she leads us forward. I smile. How beautiful you are, and how real and rough and true.

If a man is a bird, well, what then? And if a man is a man... There, my love, lies the fear.

I miss your smiles - no, I miss the way you smiled for me. I miss

you.

The trees, the books, the paints can hold my tears back, but only you can dry them once they start to fall.

My fantasies envelope me, so innocent, so pure,
until I blink one time too many and remember I
live in a broken world.

But even broken things can heal.

He Was the Sun.

He was looking at me with a hunger in his face
that boys like me learn to ignore as soon as we
can climb a tree.

I have never climbed a tree.
I was curious.

"What are you
looking for, sir?"

"If I had eyes like yours, I would have
started living years ago." I didn't

know what he meant but
I trusted him.

"What's your name?"

My mother told me never to give my
name to a fairy. My father told me never to get
too close to a man who made you feel like every
day was an adventure, never to trust a man who
made you feel like you could fly.

I suppose I was caught up in the thrill of
his honey-sweet voice and his exposed biceps.

"It's Icarus. My name is Icarus."

He leaned
closer.

"Don't get off at your stop. Stay on the
bus with me, Icarus."

I did.

His lips tasted as sweet as his voice
sounded, but he always felt like
he had a
fever
and I didn't have any way to save him. I
didn't have any way to save
myself
either.

He was gentle, at first.
But my father was right.

He made me feel like every day was an
adventure and
like I could fly.

Boys like me, boys who learn to
pray before they know
who
they're praying to,
boys who stop praying as soon as they
leave home,
can not fly.

They can kiss beautiful blond bus-ride
men
and they can bend to every whim of the
man who first told them they had eyes

like the ocean
but they can't fly.

I can't fly.
I never could.

All I could do was sit on the beach where
he left me and cry into my sunburnt hands
and realise I would never be able to enjoy
the feeling of ocean water between my
toes again.

But there's one thing they don't tell you
about boys like me, curly sun-kissed
nobody-needs-you boys, and it's that they
can grow into men who know how
to drown
in their own tears and
stand back up and
look around with their ocean eyes and see
the next adventure
and go on it.

<u>Fly Away.</u>

i. The birds were singing today.

ii. When I look out my window, the warm room feels less like a safe haven and more like a prison. I have learned to keep my blinds shut.

iii. It is better not to question it. Questions may lead to answers, and answers may lead to challenges, and challenges may lead to defeat.

iv. When man feels and expresses and learns simply for the sake of learning, that is what makes him a man. But a man is prone to tears and anguish and foolish hopes, so perhaps it is better to be something entirely nonhuman.

v. Emotion is one thing I do not understand. Emotion is one thing that cannot be put in a shiny metal box and filed away for years and years until the metal is dull and rusted. Emotion is one thing that has me convinced I am human.

vi. Perhaps if I open the blinds I will see the birds. Perhaps it is better not to know.

vii. The sound of the birds was too lovely not to look through my window. The birds were plain. Somehow, I found myself both disappointed and relieved.

viii. From now on, I will remember to keep the blinds shut.

<u>A Series of Interactions Between Two Beings of Pure Light.</u>

i. "That's him," said one. "That's the boy they call Arlo Davidson." The other was silent. Both thought it quite strange that he was called Arlo Davidson. "Such a plain name for such a special   child," said the other.

ii. The corn fields were much vaster than either of them expected. They hovered in the heavy air and wondered.

"Such a big field for such a small human," said one. The other turned around and saw a field much larger.

iii. Two men sat in a tree and kissed. The tree held both of them without complaint. The beings of light silently watched the humans. One of the beings looked at the other and realised for the first time that it didn't have lips or eyes or even hands.

"You can't kiss an orb of light," it noted.
"No," said the other.
Neither was disappointed, but both were confused.

iv. "Where is love?" asked one.
"I think you mean, 'How is love,'" said the other. They looked at one another and knew that they couldn't understand the answer even if they could figure out the question.

v. Arlo Davidson wore a quiet blue cap and a gentle, freckled face. His hair only curled in the summer and his lips only smiled late at night. Arlo Davidson stood in a dirty gas station and played the same four chords on his father's guitar. The only beings to witness him were what he thought were fireflies.

"He will change the world," said one.

"Perhaps," said the other.

vi. Arlo was not afraid when what he thought were fireflies landed in his hair. Arlo was not afraid when a small voice said,
"Good luck, Arlo Davidson."
Arlo was not afraid when what he thought were fireflies flew away.

vii. Two men climbed down from a tree. One said, "I wonder when Arlo's coming home." The other smiled and said, "Soon." As they walked inside, dozens of fireflies fluttered from the tree.

viii. When Arlo Davidson walked in the front door, both of his fathers were asleep and he was smiling. He shut the door and walked upstairs as what he thought were fireflies tried to find their way home.

ix. "Where are we?" asked one.

"'Where are we now' or 'Where are we going'?" asked the other.

"Both."

The other didn't answer.

x. Two beings of pure light hung above a tree in a forest.
"Is this home?"one wondered. The other was silent. It knew the answer was not the same for both of them.

xi. "Time will always pass," said one.
"Yes," said the other.

xii. An old man wearing a flower crown played guitar in the middle of a field and looked wistfully up at the moon. He smiled as what he thought were fireflies landed in his hair and whispered,
"Hello again, Arlo Davidson."
One looked at the other and said, "Arlo is my home."
The other flew away.
Both were at peace.

xiii. Arlo Davidson and what he thought was a firefly watched as a new star planted itself in the night sky.
"Goodbye, Arlo Davidson."
The strings of an old man's guitar hummed as one being of light joined the other.
Both were silent.
Both were home.

<u>Death is Inevitable, or, Have a Pretzel: Talks
With God.</u>

i. I look into God's fiery face and say,
        hey, dude, what's up?
and God laughs and lights a cigarette and asks if
I'd like to sit down.

ii. *We are all dying,*
                    I explain,
                                *and
nobody is sure whether death
       is a horror or a comfort.*
God smiles and nods and says nothing.

iii. God and I are sitting on the floor of a Circle K
when God leans over, almost too close, and
whispers something just quiet enough that I
can't hear it.
                Pass it on,
                     says God,
but I know nobody cares what God has to say if
the messenger is wrong, and this game of tele-
phone could never end well.

iv. I ask God,
                Do you have any regrets?
and God says,
           I never should have let there be hate.
After a moment, God says,
                *I never should have let
there be mosquitoes, either.*

God asks if I have any regrets and I laugh until I start to cry.

v. God giggles quietly and winks at me and says,
I was totally hammered when I made snakes,
and we fist bump and laugh and look up pictures of snakes on our phones.

vi. Sometimes I wonder how God can take care of this place when we spend so much time just hanging around. God is a kid, I think, and God doesn't really know how to do all the stuff a god is supposed to do.

vii. *Good luck,*

says God at our last goodbye.
Yeah, I say, *good luck.*

Adventures in Friendship With Satan.

i. Today Satan and I are at a party. Satan and I are dancing, and whenever I flirt with a pretty girl Satan catches her eye and invites her to dance. Somehow I don't mind. That's just Satan's sense of humour, and I'm used to it by now. There's a girl here with a laugh like a fairy. As much as I lust for her, I dare not risk having to watch her dance with Satan instead of me.

ii. Satan has brought me a birthday gift. It is a jack-in-the-box that crows slurs at me. I tell Satan that I hate it and Satan smiles so big I can almost forgive the gift.

iii. The school principal gives me a plus one to most school events. I always bring Satan. It's a lot more fun to get in trouble if you can honestly say Satan made you do it, and Satan always has terribly fun ideas.

iv. One time Satan and I spent a weekend at Satan's mother's beach house. We splashed each other with sea water and talked about life and Satan confessed to having a crush on God. I told Satan that it was never gonna happen, and God isn't really ready for a relationship- taking care of the whole world is too much responsibility already. Satan wasn't hurt. Satan rarely is.

v. If the underworld is anything like Satan describes it, I can't wait to go there. Everyone is gay and we party all day and Satan lets the girls kiss each other and make flower crowns. Satan says we're all good people and God is a prick for shutting us out and we get our own space when we die, our own little gay cove.

vi. I told Satan I wanted a dog and now a hellhound follows me wherever I go. I call her Rosie. I never get called slurs anymore, not even by the jack-in-the-box.

vii. When Satan and I sing karaoke, I take the low part. Satan has a lovely soprano, and I love harmonies. We always get stared at, and we always have fun.

The Laughter Chronicles.

i. He was laughing so hard she couldn't look at him. He found this hilarious.

ii. I don't know you and I never did. It is a fool who falls in love with a name and a face and a pair of hands. I am not a fool, I hope. Maybe it was your laughter that did it.

iii. Good luck finding a duck among all those giggling geese. (This one will make sense later, darling.)

iv. Knock knock.
   Who's there?
   Me. Who else visits you?
   Only the sun.

v. The fish are laughing today. I laugh with them. We all laugh together until an arrow pierces my heart.

vi. Ho ho ho, says the jolly man. Hee hee hee, he chants. He smiles a practiced sort of smile and winks.

vii. There is a girl who shines like the moon. She has stars in her hair and clouds in her eyes. She cackles kindly and jovially and is told she is ugly. Her ears disagree.

Soft Graphite, #2.

The desire burns in my fingertips, straining
against my skin, swelling and pulling my hands
closer to him

Look, don't touch

and Reason, cruel dictator of the body and mind,
Reason holds me still. I am not a human being. I
am a soul, a writing mass of emotion hidden in
this useless, awkward, fleshy prison.

You don't deserve-

I don't deserve anything, yet I have everything,
everything but him, and it's all so grand but all
so
              empty
and I can wait, I will wait for him. For nothing
will change, can change, until you want it to
stay. How can I know he wants me?

Why? Why him? Why you?

How can I answer, knowing so little, hoping so
much? How can I answer, believing I am worth-
less and he is so much more than he could be?
How can I answer, doting on him, wanting him,
silently begging for a smile, yet barely even
knowing who
or what
he is?

<u>Written on the Prison Wall.</u>

I think in verse and profanity.

I wonder if I should tell you that today I tried to drown myself in the bathtub, or that the reason I take so long to clean myself is because I'm trying to wash my own fingerprints off my body.

You don't ask, and I don't tell.

There is a glass of something blue on the counter. I wonder what would happen in I drank it, but I suppose it wouldn't matter because it wouldn't end in your hands teaching my hands what it feels like to be held and it wouldn't end in you calling me
yours.

I'll always be your girl but that doesn't mean you can touch me like that, not if you're going to move on the next morning.

I'll always be your girl, but that doesn't mean I should take the blame for the acid and the club and the last words of
Tell Sharon I've always loved her, even on the rainy days
as the sun watched and burned logic away.

I'll always be your girl but that doesn't mean you'll always be mine and that frightens me almost as much as the look in your eyes when I said
We killed him!
and you said
No, I killed him; you just get the credit.

and I didn't want the credit but you wrapped it up so looked so desirable and gave it to me all done up in happy birthday ribbon and ran away before the sirens reached us and even as my wrists bled from the handcuffs cutting into them I was yours.

And when they asked me if I killed Thomas Weiss I told them I never killed anybody, I just got the credit, but I never mentioned your name.

And when their questions zapped my brain until I didn't know my name and, even stranger, I didn't know yours, I thanked them for their patience and asked them if someone could please tell Sharon that Thomas had loved her even on the rainy days and could someone please tell me that I could go home now because I never touched the acid or the club and I never felt the pride and excitement in your eyes

In whose eyes?

they asked, and I said I'd promised not to tell.

I know you do not like it here, but I promise I never told them it was you. I've always been your girl, and I still don't know how they found you or why you hate me some, use me some, blame me always.

I wonder if I should tell you that I love you even on the rainy days. You probably wouldn't get the reference.

ive always been a good kid
golden child
made mama proud
im the kid who said bitch for the first time when
i was 18
n only then b/c i wanted 2 make u laugh
the kid who cries 2 easy n 2 long
the kid whos never late
the kid who tells mama yeah there was weed but
i didnt smoke
n the kid who means it b/c smoking isnt golden
the kid who lets u go 1st n maybe thats why i
feel like im
the kid who gets left behind

u dont have 2 respond idk if this makes any
sense

Not Quite Christmas Spirit.

i. I am laughing in a way that frightens even me.

ii. I feel so dirty, so filthy in the way that you can't wash off with soap that smells like goat's milk and lilies, in the way that can't possibly get better without getting much, much worse first.

iii. I refuse to cry
but
I also refuse to pretend I'm okay.

iv. There is a place, they have told me, where everyone is welcome and everyone is safe. I do not believe them.

v. I am holding my forehead in one hand and a pencil in the other. It is winter in this room. I am pretending to be okay. I am pretending not to cry.

vi. I am screaming now. I am screaming words that I do not know. I do not know anything. I am so tired that I cannot sleep.

vii. Why don't they love me? Why am I so low and base in their eyes?

viii. Every night I look at the stars. It is my one solace. Every night I look at the stars and cry silently until the tears freeze on my cheeks and I am certain that this is all real.

ix. Elliott.
    Elliott.
    Elliott.
    Elliott.
    Elliott.

x. Maybe it's all my own fault.

xi. As soon as we enter this world we begin dying. Every second we are closer to death. Why hide from it?

xii. Because there is more than Elliott.

xiii. Because one should not be so base and vile in their own eyes.
No.
There will always be love.

xiv. Because even if i am a blundering curse, I do not want to hurt the foolish, sweet people who love me.

xv. I am laughing in way that is quiet and new, broken but ready to heal.

xvi. I
am ready to heal.

<u>Hello, Daddy!</u>

I - PROLOGUE IN BLUE

I think I am going to
melt
and this time it's not for (him).

(the boy with his heart in his pocket) or, really,
(the boy with the empty pocket)
has finally
left
because (he) thinks (he) is a Star.
We all know that title belongs
to the girls of paisley and starlight
and to the boy with the
cucumber-mint eyes.

I am standing in a secret place- no,
I Was standing in a secret place-
ready to emerge
like any firefly at dusktime.

My heart was awake then.
My Heart
was thriving.

II - WINTER, I THINK

(the boy with the empty pocket) is
standing there with (his) wife,
who I love, and (his)

daughter, who I
love, and (his) son, who (he) should
not be allowed to love.
I am staring.
I remember I am me.
I wonder if this is a memory, or else
why This is the
moment
that's still happening.

III - THIS IS WHERE IT STOPS BEING FUZZY AND EVERYTHING IS YELLOW

"I'm for you"- which I never said
then
and he never said at all (stung by a wasp, how
could he speak,) and still
when I remember
those words are the subtitle.
"I'm for you" which was the opposite of
her blonde grinning moment
and although
we loved each other
we were not
for each other then.
"I'm for-" (the boy with the empty pocket)
was Never for me
and I hope (he) knows I am not for (him).

Lo, there came (his) daughter, all
sunshine curls,
unless it was (his) daughter, all
puddles of tulip. She was

bounding over with
her hip-hop-fly-high-brother and
every day I forced him down and
every day he stepped back up and
I was proud.
That day I was of
discipline and love. That day I was for
every one of them

except (the boy with the empty pocket)
because I Love Them
and I will not try to fill what will always be emp-
ty
with my energy.

IV - PRESENT

I think of them, my summerbirds-
My Firefly! My Little Sun! My loves!-
and I sing my love to the stars that always shine
in my sky
in Our sky
and I blow a kiss to the heavens we will all reach
for.

How to Save Your Own Life.

First, you have to decide to die. Run a bath. No matter how warm it is, you will turn the hot water up and up and up. When it starts to burn your knees you know it is warm enough. Keep the hot water on for an extra six seconds, just for good measure. You will be too hot. You will be uncomfortable. That is right.

You will hesitate, and then you will put your head under the water. You count to ten. Count to ten again. You are not drowning yet. Count to ten again. Now your lungs hurt and your eyes want to open. You will be uncomfortable. That is right. Count to ten again. This time you won't make it to ten. You will count to four and burst out of the water, breathing again. You will finish counting to ten as you sit there, naked and still surviving. You will not cry. You will feel the sting of the cool air and the creeping realisation that you just tried to drown yourself. You will be uncomfortable. That is right.

You will put two of your fingers on the soap. That's when it will hit you, when you will truly understand that this is real. Your face will become cold and slack. Now you can cry. You will whisper an apology through your tears. You splash your face with water, but do not submerge it. You will be uncomfortable. That is right.

You will slowly wash, and slowly dry yourself and slowly put on your best pajamas.You will not tell your mother what you've done. All you tell her is that you love her. She hugs you then, warmly and completely. You will be very comfortable. That is right.

<u>Windows, Doors.</u>

Today I exist in a serotonous place!
There are no knives here, and no gribbling vile
"men."
Here I have rhythm.
We beat the drum.
We beat the drum.
We plither-pop the boundless beat.
We stroke the drum with feather-fingers and the
drum forgives us.
Today I exist in a serotonous place!
This is what I say in my mind.
Sometimes it feels like a symphony
Sometimes it feels   phony
but I insist on living a peach-pebble aloe-smooth
life.
Today I plemble. Today I chaunt, I shrive.
I may be of nothing, but I MUST be of petals!
I am not afraid.
I am not afraid.
I have no reason to be afraid.
If I must I will sleep with the mellimold light on.
At night I am droopsome and I lust for rest.
At night I have no reason to be afraid.
I exist in a serotonous place.
There are no knives here, and no shruffling cruel
men.
I am safe. I can see the mellimold light.
I can sleep in serendipity.
Each moment I exist in a serotonous place.

<u>From Above.</u>

i. His chocolate curls were braided by the wind
and lit by the glow that came from within him
and he was far too beautiful to be loved by like
me, a boy with confused green eyes and cal-
loused hands.

His clear, bright eyes were wide with
wonder for a world he had seen millions of
times before, a world that somehow still seemed
new when he changed his perspective, and he
was far too pure to be touched by a boy like me,
a boy who stayed inside and swore at the televi-
sion screen and and had dirt under his finger-
nails even though he never went out to get it
there.

His soft, round face was glowing with joy
as he turned his head to face me and said,
Isn't it wonderful?
And he was far too excited to notice a boy like
me saying words like mine, or rather, he was far
too excited to realise that I was referring to him
and not the trees when I said
yes.

ii. He was nervous.
I could see in his face and in the way his hands
twitched that
he was nervous.
Suddenly I realised that I had known him for his
whole life, loved him for his whole life, and
he
had not

known me.

He was wonderfully attractive, with his curious green eyes and strong hands with just enough dirt under the fingernails so you could tell he was real.

He was a true, handsome boy, not one of those cardboard cutouts that are always clean and neat and quiet.

He was rough in all the right ways.

Yet I could not touch him.

I could not have him.

There was no way he could love me if he didn't even know me.

iii. A fool and a mortal sat in a boat and smiled, and time passed.

A fool and a mortal looked at the sun and the mortal said

You're beautiful

and

I love you

and the fool thought the sun was the recipient of these words.

A fool and a mortal fell asleep in each others' arms and the fool leaned down and kissed the mortal's forehead and wished and time continued to pass.

A fool and a mortal looked into each others' eyes and the mortal said

You're beautiful

and the fool said

I love you

and in that moment, all was well.

iv. From above, anyone could have seen it coming. But the fool and the mortal did not, and somehow that made the moment even sweeter.

<u>Psallite! Or, Have a Heart, Jerry.</u>

i. There is a woman made of sunshine and a
woman made of tears and
neither has ever heard her own name.
The woman made of sunshine is lovely to look
at, but every man who has ever loved her has
been burned.
Only the woman made of tears can touch her,
and neither would have it any other way.

ii. O! we shall sing like the songbirds!
O! We shall flap our skin-covered, bony wings as
we fall!
O glory! And a gay
HUZZAH!

iii. Something in her face drowns me. Perhaps it
is
her eyes.
If I die (which surely I will), I hope it is because I
drowned in a sweet lady's deep, warm eyes.

iv. She confuses me.
Sometimes I want
to kiss her gentle lips
and tell her she is beautiful.
Sometimes I want to tell her she's a good friend
and to know in my heart that's all she is.
And sometimes I forget she's even there.
Maybe she is my angel. Maybe I am but a fool
and she was more than I saw all along.

v. How now! An intermission! When the good people return, covered in stardust and footprints, so shall the players. Hush, children! Cue the drums!

vi. A MAN walks onstage. So does a YOU. The YOU is afraid, but the MAN says that is stupid. The MAN whips the YOU and laughs. Enter a ME. The ME begins to cry, but is too afraid to help the YOU. The MAN cackles indefinitely.

vii. Some collect seashells. The strong, dark man collects names he has been called. He has twenty-three. He might tell you of them:
(Jessica, Sweetie, Cupcake, Darling, Doll, Precious, You There, Girl, Dyke, Faggot, M'Lady, Hoe, Slut, Honey, Baby, Chickadee, Love, Girlfriend, Starshine, Poser, Liar, Tranny, Jacob)
These are neatly in order.

viii. Once I told a man I was texting The Most Beautiful Girl in the World. He was my cousin. When I told him, he didn't believe me. When I told him I loved her, it was a coward's way of saying it. I was afraid that if it was more than implied, he would not want to be my cousin anymore.
There were only two people I told that night. Another cousin, who couldn't understand but tried to support me, and the Most Beautiful Girl herself.

ix. Stop! Rewind! We musn't relive mistakes and dreams.
Let us pretend, now, that we have a balloon.
O! To let go and watch it fly! Except for the fear that then the balloon should be gone.

x. Some men are cruel. Some men are kind. Some men simply wish to make it clear that not ALL men-----! Not ALL!

xi. "Good morning!" says the sun, and lo! I begin to cry! I miss my sweet lover the moon.

xii. My body is too lumpish and my voice is too young and I will never quite be enough, I think, but my muse giggles and tells me to think, no, my body and voice must be trained! They are not wrong! Only new! And so I rejoice.

xiii. "Was that the story you wanted to hear?"
"No, my love, but it was the one I needed to hear."
"You are wiser than I knew."
And their creaking forms moved slowly into the silhouette of a kiss.

Thank you.

I would like to extend a special thank you to those who have inspired and supported me throughout not only the process of writing and publishing these poems, but my entire life. First and foremost, to my family- my love for you is at the core of my being, and I am so glad to have a family that makes me laugh, always encourages my pursuits, and is unconditionally there for me. All my love to you. Mama, your patience, enthusiasm, and wisdom has impacted every orifice of my being and I would certainly not be where I am now without your love and guidance. Thanks also for encouraging me to put in the work to get this done and for the work you did as an editor, an advisor, and my biggest supporter. I love you. Dad, I can't imagine what I'd do without your honest and optimistic outlook on life. Because of you, I am able to live in the moment but never stop moving forward. Kari, Espen, and Stine, you are by far the best siblings I could ask for. You make me laugh, you support me even when you don't fully understand what I'm so excited about, and I can always count on you to be the best of friends to me. Thanks to Mormor and Morfar for your infallible interest in my writings and my life, and to all the relatives and family friends who ask about my poems and offer a fresh interpretation along with their encouragement.

Thanks also to all the friends and mentors who have read my rough drafts and been the inspiration for so many writings. Your thought and kindness means so much to me, and I feel so lucky to have you in my life. All my love to all of you. I'd like to give a shoutout to all the teachers and librarians who helped me grow as a writer and who encouraged me to continue to write. A genuine thank you goes to Mrs. Amy Klenz for all her work as a mentor and guide as I figured out what being a poet meant to me, and for her influence on my taste in literature. Being a reader has certainly helped me as a writer! Thanks also to Mr. Geoff Friedrich for his help with my entrance into the 2017-18 Scholastic Art and Writing Awards- without you, I wouldn't have accomplished what is so far one of the highlights of my writing career.

Last but not least, I'd like to thank everyone who read this book. Being published is a longtime dream of mine, and having my work out in the world is deeply exciting to me. Thank you for helping me achieve my dream and for letting me share my words with you.

40795427R00051

Made in the USA
Lexington, KY
02 June 2019